XERISCAPING & SUSTAINABILITY FOR NEW ENGLAND

A Practical Guide
to
A Water-Wise Landscape
Using Native Plants

DIANE M. GUIDEBECK

The views and opinions contained in this work are those of the author.

Copyright© 2025 by
Diane M. Guidebeck

All rights reserved. No part of this book may be reprinted or used in any manner without written permission of the author with the exception of brief quotations for book reviews.

First Edition

All rights reserved.

Published in the United States

ISBN: 978-1-951854-46-1

Edited and formated by Stephanie Blackman,
Riverhaven Books,
Whitman, MA

DEDICATION

To my family for their love and support

INTRODUCTION

I guess you could say it all started with an article from college, and all I had was a Xerox copy. I have held on to the same article trying to find the author. Then, after many, many years, I finally have and even found a copy of the book to buy. The author, Carlton B. Lees, and the book *New Budget Landscaping*, Chapter 1 "in the beginning" started my career with the outdoor world. The author takes gardens, landscapes, and the natural environment and shows us how we can create rooms, living environments, into our own backyards. History shows how we have manipulated our taste or desire. And the planet has a way of paying us back, one way or another. So, as we turn to work with nature and not against her, let's consider how we can achieve satisfaction for ourselves and this wonderful planet we call home.

He uses words – use, comfort, pleasure, villa, area, space, outer space, organization, chaos, room, and garden – to describe the garden.

We need to understand these words to sculpt, create, and make sense of our environment or make sense of the chaos and turn it into a living area to enjoy by humans and nature.

James Rose, a landscape architect, says, "being inside a garden should be like being inside a piece of sculpture."

This book will focus on how to achieve this with low water plants to help conserve the planet's supply and still have beauty, function, form, and balance.

In 1999 as an undergrad, I wrote an article titled "Xeriscaping for New England," and until now have slowly been trying to put this book together, so here we go.

Table of Contents

Chapter 1 "Xeriscape"   1

Chapter 2 Methodology   9

Chapter 3 Maintenance/IPM   21

Chapter 4 Design and Layout   32

Chapter 5 The Seven Steps to Xeriscape   41

Chapter 6 Plants Native Style   45

APPENDIX   61

CHAPTER 1

So, what is it and how can we create something that is good for both us and the environment? There is a selection of plants known in the world as Xerophytes: a plant structurally adapted for life and growth with a limited water supply, especially by means of mechanisms that limit transpiration or that provide for the storage of water.

According to Webster Dictionary, this is derived from the Greek words XEROS, meaning dry, and PHYTES, meaning a plant having a (specified) characteristics or habitat.

ORIGINS

The origins of Xeriscape in the United States started in Colorado in early 1981. With increasing water bans, the Associated Landscape Contractors of Colorado (ALCC) and Denver Water formed a cooperative task force on water conservation. Jim Grabow the president of the ALCC and Bill Miller, manager of Denver Water, worked jointly to form a plan with the projected future of water supply in mind. With a joint task force from the green industry, educators, and blue (water) industries working to minimize water usage, communities needed guidance on ways to beautify the land urban growth and remain conscientious about water usage.

Nancy Leavitt, an Environmental Planner for Denver Water, created the word Xeriscape as a name for both the garden and education brainstorming sessions; hence the original definition of Xeriscape – "water conservation through creative landscaping" – and its seven principles began in early 1982.

There are four C's that are to be considered when you landscape, for you and the environment "so all will thrive."

XERISCAPING & SUSTAINABILITY FOR NEW ENGLAND

NEED FOR THE 4 C's

CLIMATE

What is the climate in which we live in? This can be better understood if we look at the zone map from the USDA in the appendix. In New England our zone ranges from 7a/b to 2b. The average minimum temperature difference is from 5 degrees (zone 7 a/b) Fahrenheit to -50 degrees Fahrenheit. Plants have a range on which they can grow and survive, and some do require that cold time to survive.

Vernalization is a physiological process in some plants where the flowers, or sometimes the seeds, must go through a prolonged period of cold to blossom or germinate in the spring. The amount of cold required by a plant is measured in chill hours.
www.annarbor.com/home-garden/winter-does-a-garden-good

There is a saying, "the right plant for the right place." It is very important to choose and know your zone environment. Properties can have different microclimates from the north side of the house to the south, and the amount of sun, shade, and wind can greatly affect the plant. The tags that accompany plants serve as a very useful tool in planning a landscape. This will be further explained in the design process chapter.

CONSERVATION

The word "conservation" can equal dollar signs to many people when they have to go before the conservation commission to build or renovate property. But the job of this group of people is to protect, preserve, and restore the property so society can live harmoniously with nature and not struggle against her. Science and history have shown that when attacked, Mother Nature will fight. And this is one opponent humanity cannot beat. So, if you can't beat 'em...

The protection of nature is important, plants give us the oxygen we need to breathe, and they help remove the deadly greenhouse carbon dioxide gas in the air. Plantings provide stabilization for the soil, hillsides, and banks. They also provide habitats for animals, insects, and resources of all kinds for humans. So based on your property location, you may or may not have to go through conservation to plant on your property. Please check with the local town municipality.

CARE

What is it to care for nature? It is maintenance, attention, and consideration of the landscape. This book will help you maintain the gardens with consideration to your back and to help you enjoy the landscape without becoming a slave to the yard. This book will help you to create rooms within the landscape and, like all rooms, they can be rearranged as needed. Although plants should not be moved as often as you move the sofa. Plants need to get established to survive. Careful planning is required.

CONCERN

Let's do what we can to help the present day with concern for the future. The ever-increasing water bans and the need for bottled water inform us about the direction our environment is headed. Also, just try to breathe in some parts of the world (smog, pollution, CO2) and you'll notice the ever-increasing need for space. As the saying goes "by taking care of the little things, the big things take care of themselves."

The need to keep all species of plants and animals (this includes us) in a healthy climate with care and concern for the conservation of Earth is possible. So, let's learn how to XERISCAPE.

XERISCAPING & SUSTAINABILITY FOR NEW ENGLAND

*"Take care of the small things,
The big things take care of themselves.
You can gain more control over your life by
Paying close attention to the little things."*
~ Emily Dickinson, 1830-1886

A LITTLE BOTANY

By understanding why plants are important to the environment, one must first visualize how the plant breathes, which in turn allows us to breathe. Plants take in deadly carbon dioxide (CO_2) and expel oxygen (O) and water (H_2O) as the diagram shows:

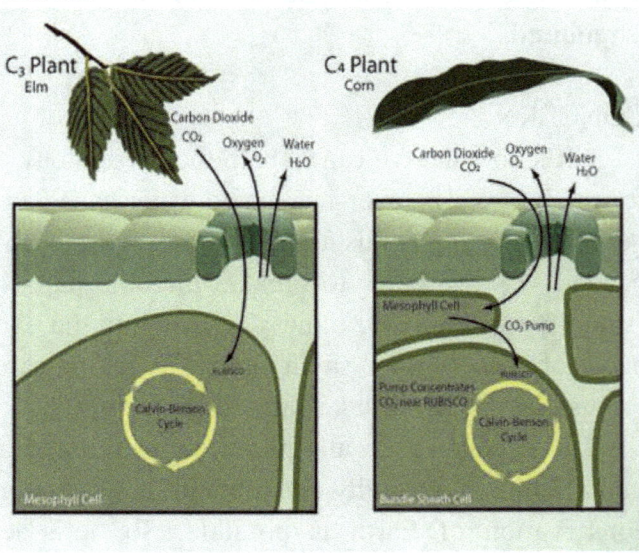

www.skepticalscience.com

This is one reason why planting material that is more suited for the environment when limited water is needed or available is vital.

What is the difference between C3 and C4 plants? The first difference is in the thickness of the leaves. The C4 are a generally thicker walled structure, which help it to hold onto water better. This protects the plant from drying out quicker in hot conditions. It also has the ability to better adapt to environments of low CO_2 levels and modify its photosynthesis process.

Based on the environment all plants have a place.

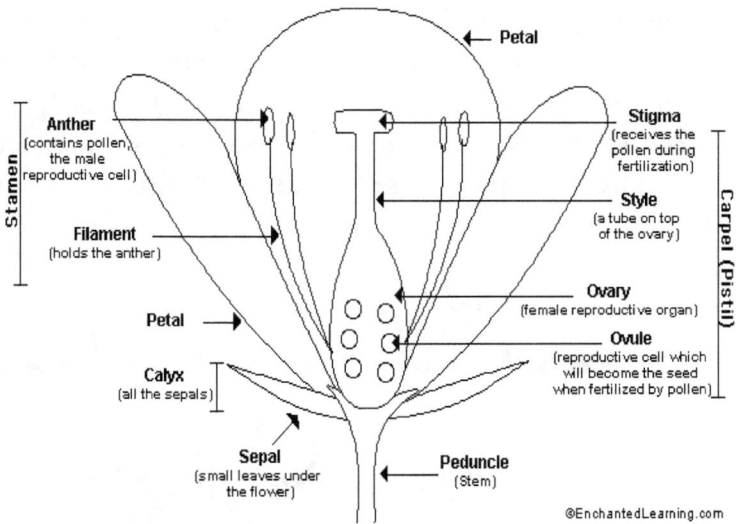

Whether a plant flowers or not is important. Flowering plants, trees, and shrubs also serve multiple purposes. First, they serve as food for insects and animals, generally through the pollen or nectar on the flower. The pollen is actually the male part of the flower (the diagram labels it as the STAMEN), and the insect or animal will feed on this and/or carry some of it to the next flower. This pollen is then transferred to the female part of the plant, the CARPEL (PISTEL), that pollinates the plant's reproductive process. Thank God for the birds and the bees.

SUSTAINABILITY

Sustainability is a word often used in landscaping by the United Nations. Their goal is "Meeting the needs of the present without compromising the ability of future generations to meet their own needs" (social, economic, etc.). This includes being good stewards because we must ensure "that future generations can meet their own needs without being deprived of the resources and opportunities necessary for their well-being." Sustainability of the environment and the soil, where more life lives, is vitally important to beauty and health above the ground.

One teaspoon of soil contains more living organisms than there are people in the world. James Hutton Institute

A single teaspoon (1 gram) of rich garden soil can hold up to one billion bacteria, several yards of fungal filaments, several thousand protozoa, and scores of nematodes, according to Kathy Merrifield, a retired nematologist at Oregon State University.

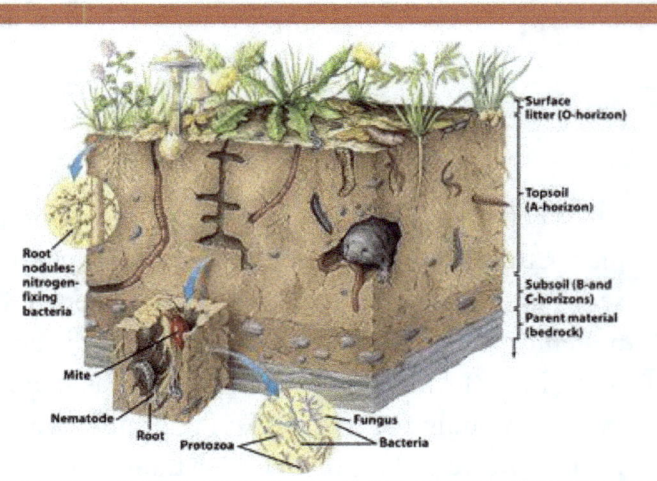

https://cwppra.wordpress.com/wp-content/uploads/2018/03/soil-organism_ww.jpg

Key principles of environmental sustainability include:

1. Conservation of Resources: Irrigation, watering using Xeriscaping, rain barrels.
2. Reduction of Waste: Minimizing waste generation, promoting recycling, and reducing pollution and composting.
3. Biodiversity Preservation: Protecting ecosystems and species to maintain a balanced and healthy environment. Using pollinators and other habitats for survival.
4. Sustainable Practices in Agriculture, Industry, and Development: Ensuring that farming, manufacturing, and construction practices are environmentally responsible and energy efficient.
5. Know Your Environment: Analyze all aspects of what your water needs are and the availability of resources. What are your shade/sun conditions?

How to use environmental sustainability in your life:

1. Reduce, Reuse, Recycle: Minimize waste by buying only what you need, reusing items, and recycling materials. Cardboard and newspaper are great for adding a weed layer to non-vegetable beds.
2. Support Eco-friendly Products: Choose products made with sustainable materials or from companies that prioritize environmental responsibility. For me it is Espoma Biotone Starter plus, which I use to plant with and amend plants during the season by raking it into the soil.
3. Conserve Water: Use water-efficient appliances, take shorter showers, and fix leaks promptly. Utilize rain barrels, and amend soil by adding compost and thin layers of mulch.
4. Plant Trees and Support Conservation Efforts: Participate in local environmental efforts and support conservation initiatives.

5.Planting of Native species: Check with your local state, extension office, and universities. Your local nursery and garden centers have sections to promote native plants, and plant tags have this information also.

6.Educate and Advocate: Spread awareness and encourage sustainable practices within your community. Home Owner Associations are starting to embrace sustainability as it helps reduce watering and improves the neighborhood.

7.Soil Test: Local universities or Master Gardeners can help improve your soil either in lawns or gardens (vegetable or flower garden). For more information, use sources such as https://ag.umass.edu/services/soil-plant-nutrient-testing-laboratory/ordering-information-forms.

8.Use companion plantings which help each other out. One example is planting any Allium in with Roses; over time, this makes the plant more fragrant and bug repellent. Another pairing is that Rhododendrons love to be planted with Mountain Laurels.

By incorporating these actions into your daily life, you can contribute to the broader goal of environmental sustainability and help mitigate the effects of climate change and resource depletion.

DIANE M. GUIDEBECK

CHAPTER 2

METHODOLOGY

There are a few basics that may come in handy when working on the earth. Both by its definition and terminology one can understand.

THE LOWDOWN ON DIRT

RULE #1 not all soil is equal.

The proper pronunciation varies, just don't call it dirt. So, what is loam (aka soil)? It is made up of three components (soil triangle): <u>clay</u> which is of a slimy consistency when wet, <u>sand</u> gritty in texture, <u>silt</u> is a fine powder (rock dust) consistency. The percentage of each is what gives loam its texture, properties and consistency for planting. The thicker the layer of loam,

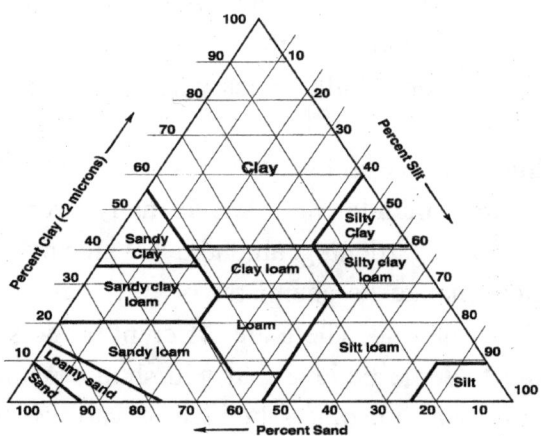

either in plant beds or lawn, aid in establishing a deeper root system and less water is generally required.

A good method to test the cohesiveness of your loam is to

do a ribbon test. This is when you have a small ball of moist loam in your hand and roll it between your fingers to approximately ¼" ribbon. It should hold together. If it breaks down, it has too much sand in the mix. If it is too stiff and slimy, it has too much clay in the mix.

It should also have a pleasant earthy smell to it; if it has a foul odor, it is likely there is a problem with the soil. For instance, it could be anaerobic soil (no oxygen), which means the soil is not living. Or it could also be a fungus or bacteria in the soil which could potentially be dangerous to the plant. The soil is a living organism with good fungus and bacteria to help breakdown fertilizer and microbes to add to the plant as it grows and gets nutrients.

Now, we can buy "soil" in bags; topsoil is exactly that – the first twelve inches of the earth which consists of the existing vegetation matter of the area. It can be a variety of clay, sand, silt, and other matter. A typical soil is made up of less than 52% sand (which is great for drainage), 28-50% silt (which is used for increased fertility and moisture retainage), and >20% clay (which is great for moisture retainage). The chart in the appendix shows and gives the variety of blends of loam. When buying in bags or in bulk, check what you are buying.

Amendments to the soil vary

What are amendments? While many people think of the Constitution, in gardening, amendments are any additions to the soil which change its chemistry or physical nature. Are they needed? Yes and no. There are different schools of thought on this subject. Some believe that you should plant in the soil a plant is to grow in, others believe to various degrees to add amendments.

By not amending the soil, the plant adapts to the existing conditions and grows on what is available. This can work in natural settings, but if the alternative look is desired, then one must add amendments. It is believed some degree of amendments is required to get the plants established. Research has shown the addition of beneficial bacteria with small amounts of organic matter and fertilizer get the soil working as well as the plant to ensure success. This and water, water, water.

RULE#2 less is more.
The theory to add more fertilizer or amendments will not work; you will burn the plant and its roots. It is better to use a small amount over time than to shock the plant. So, what are amendments?
1. Organic matter – a soil that consists of plant and animal residue.
    a. Plants – roots, leaves …. all finely ground
    b. Animal – manure, sludge (sewage) not for vegetable or edible crops.
    * A good percentage is 2-4% organic matter in the soil.
2. Humus is highly decomposed organic matter.

Organic matter can be made by composting in one's yard (except for the sludge, please leave that for the professionals). Composting can be done by using lawn clippings, leaves, vegetable scraps, and garden waste by layering in either a pre-made bin or self-made bin. It can even be done on pallets or in a cleared area in the back of the yard. It must get some sunlight and have access to some moisture. Do not use meat or dairy products. I equate composting to a diet which requires protein and carbohydrates. The protein is your green leafy items; this is what generates the heat to break down the carbohydrates. The carbohydrates are all your brown material. The percentage of protein to carbohydrates is 25 % protein to 75 % carbohydrates; this percentage can vary based on location, sun, moisture, and how often the pile can be turned for proper air circulation. The heat generated from the compost pile, if done properly, will destroy some pathogens and weed seeds. The optimum temperature for the compost pile is 150° Fahrenheit, not to exceed 165° F or below 135° F; at these temperatures the compost is not working properly.

A good policy to practice is having the soil tested by your local extension service or university with a horticulture program. Sometimes annually is good until things are in balance. The costs are generally affordable, jut be honest with what you are growing or planning on growing. They will give you recommendations on what to add or not add to the soil. They will test nutrients, pH, and any organic matter in the soil.

NUTRIENTS

There are macronutrients in the soil as well as micronutrients. These are subject to pH levels in the soil. All living things require food to grow; plants require nutrients to grow also. There are three major nutrients: N-P-K, which stand for nitrogen (N), phosphorus (P), and potassium (K). Each serves a distinctive purpose in the plant's food cycle. Other major elements needed by plants are oxygen, carbon, and hydrogen, which are needed in photosynthesis.

Nitrogen is an essential macronutrient used to generate amino acids and proteins, genetic material, chlorophyll, and other important molecules. It serves to green the plant and aid in initial growth.

Phosphorus helps the plant on a cellular level and its energy system. It also helps the plants develop flowers and strengthen the root system. This is especially critical for lawns going into winter's dormant state.

Potassium (Potash) is essential for the plant's overall health. The micronutrients contribute to plants' overall health. The micronutrients are boron (B), copper (Cu), iron (Fe), chloride (Cl), manganese (Mn), molybdenum (Mo), and zinc (Zn). These are also included in your soil report. I have enclosed a sample of a report from the local University.

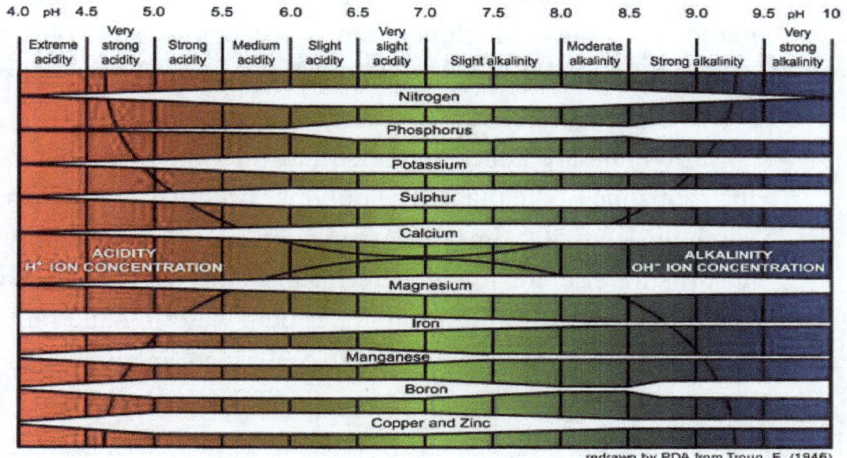

WATER

Water is everywhere and not a drop for my garden. This is sometimes apparent during drought season or maybe year-round depending on rainfall. This is why either incorporating or doing Xeriscape is needed. There are many alternatives to watering a garden, lawn, or crop. Check with your local municipality and building department for regulations.

Rain barrels have been around (no pun intended) collecting water from roofs and gutters. The elevated rain barrel is drained through a spicket or spigot in the bottom of the barrel. I have hooked these up to a complete irrigation system with success. Work with the irrigation person and you both can learn something new.

Cisterns are underground or above-ground waterproof containers to hold water for later usage. The water is delivered by pipes from a pump in the cistern. If the cistern is above the area to be watered, it can be gravity fed.

Gray Water is the discharge water from the washing machine, dishwasher, showers, and sinks. This can be used for lawns, shrubs, and trees. Using this in fruit trees and vegetable gardens is a personal choice, but is acceptable only if the grey water does not come in contact with the crop. Storage of grey water is not recommended.

Polymers are added to the soil at the time of planting into the root zone of the plant. The polymer becomes gelatinous and can hold 10 to 500 times its own weight in water. The polymer absorbs water in the initial watering and slowly the plant's roots feed off this moisture. Through periodic watering and rain, the plant gets the needed moisture. So, your watering is reduced by about 50%.

MULCH

What is mulch and why care what type is used? Mulch is used both for aesthetic purposes and for weed control. It also protects the plant's root zone and helps retain moisture in the soil. Over time true bark mulch will break down and provide organic matter back into the soil. According to Merriam-Webster Dictionary (still old school), mulch by its definition is: *a protective covering (as of sawdust, compost, or paper) spread or left on the ground to reduce evaporation, maintain even soil temperature, prevent erosion, control weeds, enrich the soil, or keep fruit (as strawberries) clean.*

The different types that can be used are at the owner's discretion and final purpose.

- Leaf Compost – this is a great way to use the leaves from yard cleanup and grind them up and place them around plants. The only concern is the types of leaves used on Cape Cod. Our Oak leaves have a high pH value and tannic, which can burn delicate plants. This can also alter the pH in the soil and the plant may not do well. So it is important to know your plant and how to care for each. Leaf Compost has many benefits to gardens, but sourcing can be difficult.

- Bark Mulch – is made from the outer layer of the tree at harvest. The product is shredded and ground to various contents.
- Wood Chips – are made from the inner part of the tree and ground to various sizes or chunks.
- Man-made Mulch – this can vary from rubber to plastic and be dyed to almost any color desired.
- Dyed Mulch – this is generally made from bark mulch or wood chips. The dye that is used is non-toxic, but in my observation over the past 20 years it does not break down into the soil. I call this Nuclear Mulch.
- Peat Moss – acceptable in thin layers but then one must worry about it blowing away and retaining too much moisture. Peat Moss harvesting has been determined to release cardon dioxide (CO^2) into the environment, a major contributor to climate problems. It also destroys habitats.
- Stone – this never breaks down, but the labor saved in replacing it is worth it. It is not for every area, but the visual look is quite rich and striking. It works well in shrub and tree beds. It also provides great drainage to the plant.

Some people prefer just a thin compost layer which works very well also. Once a garden is weeded and maintained, this is acceptable, especially in perennial, annual, and vegetable gardens.

It is generally recommended to apply 3-4 inches of mulch; this can be thick depending on the type of material used. I am a

1–2-inch believer and have experienced, if done properly, plants will thrive. You do not want to suffocate the plant, as no water or air can get through. It is also recommended not to pile mulch near the trunk or stems of plants as this can burn them, depending on the material. This leaves the plant suffocating and developing only feeder roots within the mulch and trunk. No stabilizer or secondary roots will form and the tree dies from the top down.

Proper transplanting, mulching and planting will be outlaid further in this book.

RULE #3 no volcano mulch (you know who you are)
(Can you find the root flare ?)

https://extension.unh.edu/sites/default/files/styles/max_width_1200px/public/migrated_images/volcano%20mulch%20%282%29.webp?itok=MrvOLv6G

COMPOST

Composting is a natural process that turns organic waste into nutrient-rich soil for your garden. Here is a simple guide to get you started:

1. Choose a Composting Method – There are many ways to achieve nutrient-rich compost, depending on your space and resources:
    - Compost bin: A closed container to hold materials; good for small spaces or if you want to contain odors.

- Compost pile: A more open approach; good for larger areas. This can be made with pallets, cinder blocks, and other materials.
- Tumbler: A rotating drum that helps speed up the composting process.
- Kitchen compost containers and bags: A way to start and add to existing piles; best to collect daily and add to outdoor pile.

2. Gather Materials

* THERE IS A MAJOR NO-NO TO ADD TO THE COMPOST – NO MEAT OR FATS/OILS AND NO DAIRY.
** Avoid composting diseased plants, weed seeds, and pet waste, as these can cause odors or introduce harmful bacteria.

You need both brown and green materials with a ratio of 2 parts brown _to 1 part green, which provides heat for breakdown.

Brown materials (carbon-rich) provide structure and help aerate the pile.

o Leaves
o Straw or hay
o Shredded paper or cardboard
o Sawdust (from untreated wood)
o Small branches or twigs

Green materials (nitrogen-rich) provide moisture and nutrients.

o Fruit and vegetable scraps
o Grass clippings
o Coffee grounds
o Eggshells
o Plant trimmings
o Manure from herbivores (chickens, cows, etc.)

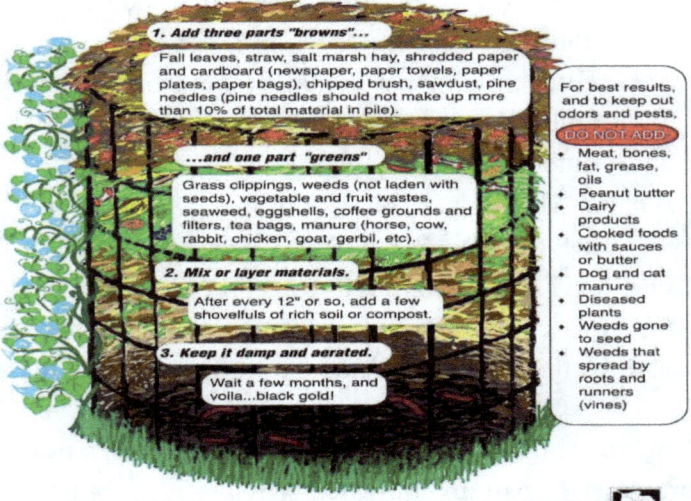

https://www.mass.gov/doc/poster-composting-is-easy/download

3. How to Create Layers
- Start with a layer of course, brown materials (e.g. small twigs or straw) at the bottom. This helps with air circulation.
- Alternate layers of green and brown materials, aiming for about two parts brown to one part green.
- Chop or shred larger materials (like cardboard or branches) to speed up decomposition.

4. Maintain Your Pile
- Aerate: Turn the compost pile regularly (every 2-3 weeks) with a pitchfork or compost aerator. This ensures oxygen reaches the microorganisms that break down the material.
- Moisture: Your compost should be as moist as a wrung-out sponge. Add water if it is too dry or more dry material if it is too wet.
- Temperature is very critical for decomposing material.

Maintain your compost between 90 - 140 degrees Fahrenheit. Pathogens in this range will be killed. Above 160 degrees, compost can become sterile.

5. Let It Break Down
- Over time, microorganisms, worms, and other creatures break down the materials.
- The process can take 2-6 months depending on the size of your pile, the material, and how often you turn it.

6. Finished Compost
- When your compost is dark, crumbly, and smells earthy (not rotten), it is ready to use. It should look and feel like rich, dark soil.
- Use your compost in garden beds, flowerpots, or to enrich your lawn.

Tips:
- Smaller pieces decompose faster. Breaking down large items will speed up the process.
- If you have a compost bin, be mindful of the lid. Make sure it is not too tightly sealed in order to allow airflow.

With patience, you will have your own homemade compost, which will enhance the health of your plants!

From scraps to GOLD

www.istock.com

Now is a good time to pause and ask yourself a few questions:

What is your final purpose? Be very honest about what you wish to achieve and what that will require.
How much time will be necessary to achieve your goals?
Are there limitations to funding costs/budget?
What site work/preparation needs to be done?
Why are you doing this? To relax, play, putter?

If you are still committed, let's continue.

CHAPTER 3

Maintenance-IPM-Organic

<u>Rule # 4 the right plant in the right place</u>.

Once a garden or landscape is planted, it must be maintained. There is no such thing as a no maintenance landscape. The amount of maintenance you have to do depends on the plan and your commitment to care for the landscape. It can be a low-maintenance landscape, but with everything there is a cost. You will have done some work, just not a constant chore. Can you have the golf course lawn weed free? Sure, but not without higher labor costs and fertilizers. So, is there a happy medium? I think so, through careful planning.

Now some basics in order to care for your landscape. As with any living thing, if everything is in balance, then all will be well. In the environment there are three basic things that, if not in check, can create the perfect disease triangle.

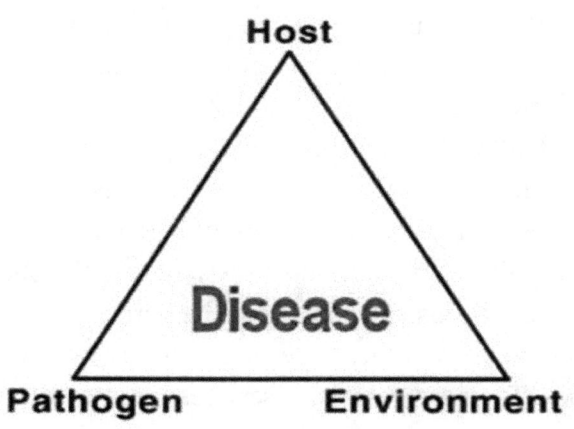

www.researchgate.net

The host is your plant, tree, or shrub. The pathogen is the actual insect, fungi, bacteria, or pathogen. The environment is the growing condition, weather, or other factors. For instance, if the environment is overly moist and the host is in distress from this, a pathogen will find the host and move right on in, uninvited. If the host is not properly fertilized and drought or wet conditions persist, things can happen. So, by keeping the triangle in balance, all will be well. Growing healthy plants will keep the pathogens at bay. There will always be some pests and pathogens in the garden, but your threshold of acceptance is how to best deal with them. This is why IPM (Integrated Pest Management) works very well. So, what is IPM? It is based on four factors: identification, monitoring, prevention, and cultural controls.

1. Identify your pest correctly – knowing the guilty party will help determine what the next step will be in control.
2. Scouting – by walking the garden/yard. I used to do this at the end of the day with a cup of coffee to see how things are doing and maybe do a little maintenance in the process.
3. Prevention – by keeping plants healthy and growing conditions favorable for the plant, problems can be prevented.
4. Cultural Controls – using chemical, biological, physical, and mechanical controls – or sometimes a combination of controls will work. The ability of the pathogen to build up a resistance to the chemical is why pathogens can sometimes be hard to control.

The use of your local extension service can be your best tool to a garden. They generally have services from soil pH testing to *what is going on in my garden* help. Most have a Master Gardener's program which answers phone calls or radio call-in shows.

IS THIS A WEED OR A FLOWER?

I had a college professor who said "A weed is nothing but an undesirable flower." I have seen some beautiful weeds and ugly flowers, so go figure. It is your final decision in your yard.

COMPANION PLANTINGS

It takes more than good soil, sun, and nutrients to ensure success in a garden. Plants must grow well with one another, and those that do are known as companions. A great book on this topic is by Bob Flowerdew, *A Guide to Gardening with Plants That Help Each Other*.

In nature, companion plants are the norm. For example:
- Blueberries, mountain laurel, azaleas, and other ericaceous (heath family) plants thrive in the acidic soils created by pines and oaks.
- Shade-loving plants seek the shelter provided by a wooded grove. The shade-lovers in return protect the forest floor from erosion with their thick tangle of shallow roots.
- Legumes and some trees, such as alders, have symbiotic relationships with bacteria in the soil that help them to capture nitrogen from the air and convert it to fertilizer, enriching the soil so plants can prosper in their presence.

Today, we recognize many plant companions. Here are some useful tips for your vegetable garden because some plants, especially herbs, act as repellents, confusing insects with their strong odors that mask the scent of the intended host plants.
- Dill and basil planted among tomatoes protect the tomatoes from hornworms, and sage scattered about the cabbage patch reduces injury from cabbage moths.
- Marigolds are as good as gold when grown with just about any garden plant, repelling beetles, nematodes, and even animal pests.

- Some companions act as trap plants, luring insects to themselves. Nasturtiums, for example, are so favored by aphids that the devastating insects will flock to them instead of other plants.
- Carrots, dill, parsley, and parsnip attract garden heroes – praying mantises, ladybugs, and spiders – that dine on insect pests.
- Much of companion planting is common sense: Lettuce, radishes, and other quick-growing plants sown between hills of melons or winter squash will mature and be harvested long before these vines need more leg room.
- Leafy greens like spinach and Swiss chard thrive when grown in the shadow of corn.
- Sunflowers appreciate the dapple shade that corn casts and, since their roots occupy different levels in the soil, don't compete for water and nutrients.

Just as some people seem to rub each other the wrong way, many plants are incompatible with one another. These plants are known as combatants or antagonists.

- While white garlic and onions repel a plethora of pests and make excellent neighbors for most garden plants, the growth of beans and peas is stunted in their presence.
- Potatoes and beans grow poorly in the company of sunflowers and, although cabbage and cauliflower are closely related, they don't like each other at all.

Sometimes plants may be helpful to one another only at a certain stage of their growth. The number and ratio of different plants growing together is often a factor in their compatibility, and sometimes plants make good companions for no apparent reason.

- You would assume that keeping a garden weed-free would be a good thing, but this is not always the case. Certain weeds pull nutrients from deep in the soil and

bring them close to the surface. When the weeds die and decompose, nutrients become available in the surface soil and are more easily accessed by shallow-rooted plants.
- Perhaps one of the most intriguing examples of strange garden bedfellows is the relationship between the weed stinging nettle and several vegetable varieties. For reasons that are unclear, plants grown in the presence of stinging nettle display exceptional vigor and resist spoiling.

One of the keys to successful companion planting is observation. Record your plant combinations and the results from year to year and share this information with other gardening friends. Companionship is just as important for gardeners as it is for gardens.

ROOT SYSTEMS AND THEIR IMPORTANCE

While all have the same purpose, not all roots perform the same job. They are for stabilizing the plant, but they are also for transporting water and nutrients into and out of the plant.

https://marvel-b1-cdn.bc0a.com/f00000000212090/aplustree.com/wp-content/uploads/2021/03/root_types-768x349.png

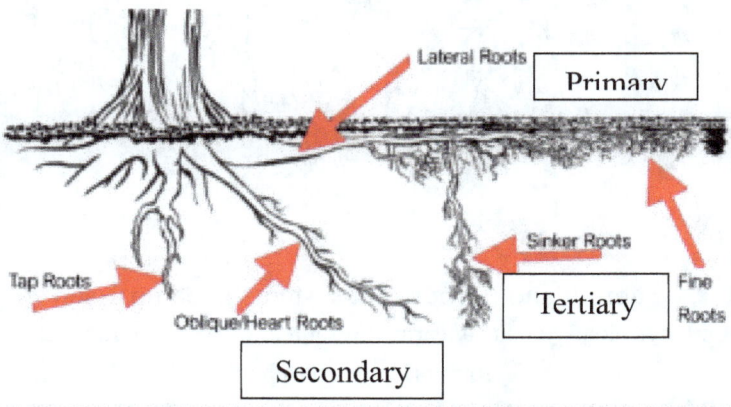

1.Tap roots: Every tree starts with a tap root that provides

stability and absorption. Over time, other roots outgrow the taproot. Most taproots don't continue to grow ever more deeply because deep soils lack the oxygen and nutrients that roots need to survive.

2. Lateral roots grow outwards right under the soil surface. They absorb a lot of water and nutrients as well as anchoring the tree.

3. Oblique/heart roots: grow at a diagonal and have the same function as lateral roots.

4. Sinker roots: grow downwards from the lateral roots to a depth of several feet. There, lateral roots take advantage of any water and nutrients deeper in the soil in addition to increasing tree stability.

5. Fine roots: All the root types aforesaid can give rise to fine roots, which is where water and nutrients are directly absorbed. They also house mycorrhizae, which are fungal partnerships that increase root absorption capacity.

https://aplustree.com/

Taproot and fibrous root systems in comparison
(http://bugs.bio.usyd.edu.au/learning/resources/plant_form_function1/plant_form/primary_roots.html).

HERBACEOUS-NON-HERBACEOUS PLANTS

Transplanting and planting a herbaceous plant involves a

few simple but key steps. Here's a guide to help you with the process:

1. Choose the Right Time
   - The best time to transplant or plant herbaceous plants is during their dormancy (fall or early spring), depending on the specific plant. Early spring is often ideal because the weather is milder and the plant will have time to establish roots before the growing season begins. Sometimes we have no choice.
   - *CALL DIG SAFE #811 before you dig.*

2. Prepare the New Location DISTURBED SOIL (takes 5-10 years to settle/compact) is susceptible to erosion OR UN-DISTRUBED (natural) SOIL, Natural Compaction is best.
   - Select a spot with the appropriate soil and light conditions for the specific herbaceous plant. Make sure the soil is well-draining, and, if necessary, amend it with compost or other organic matter to improve fertility.
   - Dig a hole that's about 1.5 to 2 times the size of the plant's root ball. The hole should be deep enough to accommodate the roots without crowding.

3. Water the Plant Before Transplanting; you can also buy WILT PRUF at your local garden center. BE MINDFUL OF WEIGHT
   - Water the herbaceous plant well a few hours before transplanting. This will make it easier to remove from its current location and reduce transplant shock.

4. Dig Up the Plant (if Transplanting)
   - Gently dig around the plant, starting a few inches from the base. Lift the plant carefully, trying to keep as many roots intact as possible. Use a spade or shovel to loosen the soil and gently lift the plant out.

5. Prepare the Plant either by ROOT PRUNE, SCORE POTTED PLANTS, ESPOMA BIOTONE STARTER PLUS

Fig. 2 & Fig, 3
- Trim any dead or damaged foliage, but avoid cutting back healthy growth unless the plant is very large and needs to be divided.
- The root system is like a straw being compressed, so if it is damaged, nothing will go in or out. Use a sharp pruner to get a clean cut just behind the damaged root.

6. Planting the Herbaceous Plant Fig. 1
- Place the plant in the hole you prepared, making sure the top of the plant is level with the surrounding soil.
- Fill the hole back in with soil and fertilizer, gently pressing it around the roots too
- If the plant is too big, you can divide it by cutting through the plant with a sharp knife. Eliminate air pockets.

7. Watering and Mulching WATERING IS A GREAT WAY TO COMPACT SOIL. Water the plant thoroughly to help settle the soil around the roots.
- After planting, give the herbaceous plant another good watering to help it adjust. You can also add a layer of mulch around the base of the plant to retain moisture, suppress weeds, and keep the soil temperature consistent.

MULCH DIAGRAM FROM FIG. 1

8. Post-Planting Care
- Keep the soil consistently moist but not soggy, especially during the first few weeks as the plant gets established.
- Monitor the plant for any signs of stress, pests, or disease. If needed, you can support the plant with stakes or other structures.

9. Staking
- Research shows and experience confirms plants create

a dependency on stakes after one year. Trees need to move and sway to set the root system into play.

This process will help the herbaceous plants settle into its new home and thrive in its new environment! Are you transplanting a specific type of herbaceous plant?

First confirm location of Root Flare. FIG. 1

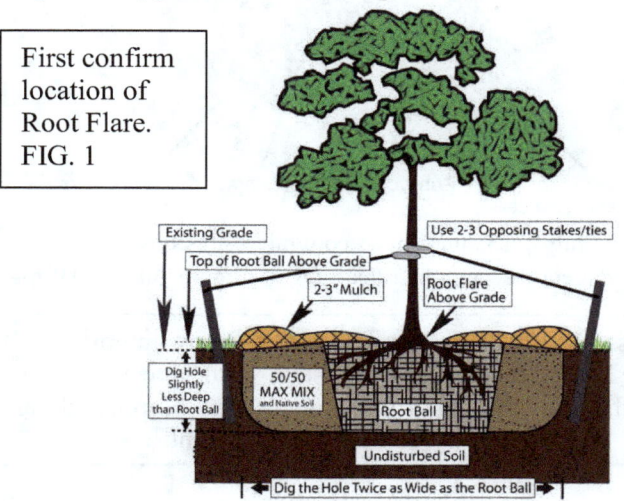

https://grasspad.com/wp-content/uploads/2020/01/tree-planting-image-Updated-Final-1000x675.jpg

Fig. 2 - Potted plants need to be scored along the sides and bottom of plant. This loosens up compressed roots sitting in the pot.

Lowes.com

XERISCAPING & SUSTAINABILITY FOR NEW ENGLAND

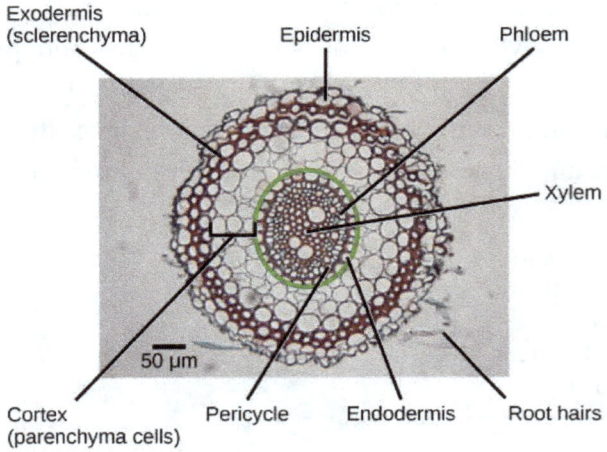

https://s3.amazonaws.com/microsite-cuny-prod/media/courseware/openstax/m66598/Figure_30_03_03f.jpg

Fig. 3 - Cross Section of a tree root – showing how important a role it plays in the health of the tree. The system starts here and extends all the way up the tree. The root pruning opens any compressed transport system UP and DOWN the plant.

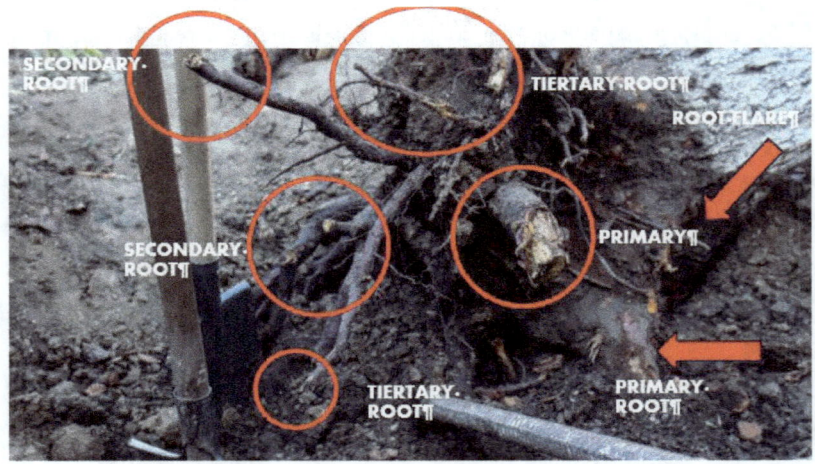

Photo: undefined undefined / iStock / Getty Images Plus / Getty Images
Fig. 4

DIANE M. GUIDEBECK

A HAPPY TREE

http://www.dirtdoctor.com/pics/content_img.1195.img.jpg

CHAPTER 4

DESIGN

So how does one go about designing a yard? As I was teaching a continuing education class, I had to figure out a way to teach landscape design. For many of us who design, we have a process we run through in our heads. How do you teach that? I put my process into a form. I use this in either designing or assessing a property for work. It is also advisable to check with your state and extension service for an invasive plant lists. Some states have put plants on this list because of their destructive nature to the local plant community. And some plants cannot be transported over state lines.

THE SEVEN STEPS (see design checklist)
1. Make a plan.
    Light requirements and conditions
    Soil conditions
    Water source
    Slope terrain
    Natural elements
2. Work the soil.
    Water capacity
    Soil texture (see soil triangle)
    Clay – smooth, sticky, forms ribbons when pressed, absorbs <1/4" per hour, but retains very well
    Loam – smooth, silky, little gritty and sticky, forms ball which fall apart easily, absorbs ¼ to ½" per hour, taken up easily by plants (sand, silt, clay)
    Sandy – loose and gritty absorbs >2" per hour, no retention by plants or soil.

Nutrients – pH level (see chart)

Amendments
Organic matter
New technology
Pure humic acid (agriculture)
Surfactants
Polyacrylamides

3. Reduce or replace lawn.
4. Plants of beauty and durability
5. Low maintenance
a. Gadgets
b. Back pain
c. Ecosystem
d. Sustainability
6. Mulch
7. Irrigation
Drip
Cisterns
Gray water, rain barrels
Polymers, anti-desiccants

XERISCAPING & SUSTAINABILITY FOR NEW ENGLAND

SITE/DESIGN CHECKLIST

Date_____Digsafe yes/no
Season_____Reference #_____

SITE ANALYSIS
*COMPASS LAYOUT   *north southeast or west*

_____

front, sides, back.
*LIGHT *filtered full partial*_____

PERCENTAGE _____

WATER TABLE *well, municipality* _____

SOURCE SUPPLIER *town, MWRA or other* _____

*NUTRIENTS (available) *this is where soil tests will give you the information needed*_____

_____

IS AREA ACIDIC/ALKALINE _____ PH_____

*SOIL *what is there now?* _____
    forest, urban, fill, farm, outwash, rocky

*ENVIRONMENTAL FACTORS *what do you see*

_____

*WIND_____ (high, low, constant, uphill, vortex)

DIRECTION_____

DIANE M. GUIDEBECK

*ADJOINING AREAS *neighbors, buildings, etc*

_____

*SQUARE FOOTAGE_____

DESCRIPTION
lawn area, garden area, play, patio, etc…….

INTENTION – PRESENT – 5 YEAR – 10 YEARS FOR DESIGN OF YOUR ROOMS-GARDEN-LAND

*COST/ESTIMATE_____

*YOUR BUDGET_____

*PURPOSE/USE *rooms, landscape, structures*
_____
formal, play, informal, cutting,
low maintenance, native, conservation

*SEASON OF INTEREST *when do you want to enjoy some or all*

_____

*IRRIGATION *how will it be done?*
hand, mechanical, chemical

_____

*MAINTENANCE_____
high, low, cleanup, cost/budget for

CRITERIA (likes/dislikes)
BALANCE, SCALE, RHYTHM,

XERISCAPING & SUSTAINABILITY FOR NEW ENGLAND

SYMMETRICAL, ASYMETRICAL

*FOCAL POINT _____

*COLOR(S) _____

*FORM(S) _____

*TEXTURE(S)_____

*EVERGREEN/DECIDUIOUS _____

TYPE_____

*TALL/SHORT/DWARF/WIDE/SLENDER_____
            screen, hedge, border, etc.

*FRAGRANCE _____

*ALLERGIES_____

*HARDSCAPES_____

DIANE M. GUIDEBECK

PLANT SELECTION: CURRENT INVENTORY

Plant	Quantity

XERISCAPING & SUSTAINABILITY FOR NEW ENGLAND

NEW PLANT SELECTION

Plant	Quantity	Cost

DIANE M. GUIDEBECK

PLAN – DRAWN yes/no

PLANTING PLAN

PHASES –YES/NO T*o be done over time? How much time?*

_____

METHOD _____
Back to front, large to small

EQUIPMENT_____

SOIL AMENDMENTS
_____

MULCH_____

MAINTENANCE PLAN
_____
_____
_____
_____
_____
_____
_____
_____
_____
_____
_____
_____
_____

FERTILIZING REQUIREMENTS _____

XERISCAPING & SUSTAINABILITY FOR NEW ENGLAND

SKETCH FOR AREA _____

DIANE M. GUIDEBECK

CHAPTER 5

Xeriscape Original Paper in 1998 (printed here as original)

<u>XERISCAPING FOR NEW ENGLAND</u>
By: Diane M. Guidebeck

So you have high water bills, would you like to lower those bills? This can be done during peak watering times and still maintain a beautiful garden, how so? Then Xeriscaping is for you. This is not a new form of gardening; just the name is new to New England. The word is a derivative of xerophytes and landscaping. Xerophytes are a group of plants which are adapted to a limited amount of water supply and store water better. This may sound of a lot to accept, but with a little practice, patience and common sense your garden will be the talk of all who pass by.

Given the reality of increasing water costs and limited water supply due to dry winters or whatever the reason, it makes sense to let Mother Nature help in achieving a once costly task in keeping everything green and alive. The gardening practice of environments of the southwest and west coast can be adapted to New England and the good news is it can be done with local native species. This form of gardening has a proven record of success in those arid regions with high water costs.

It is relatively simple to have a natural landscape with low maintains costs and still have the proper flow within the garden of color, form and texture. This according to Garden Gate (June 1996) is done by seven simple steps.

1. <u>Make a plan</u> of the yard and indicate light, shading and slope habits. Then mark the area of the desired garden by water

habits of each garden i.e.; very-low, moderate water habits and areas requiring heavier water habits. These areas should be kept small and close to the water source.

2. <u>Work the soil</u> for this area has a great impact on the plants health, so the soil should be nutrient rich and hold water adequately, but not soggy. The drainage of the soil is very important. The soil can be improved by working in humus, compost, clay and manure till the soil is rich and has good water retention without being soggy (who wants soggy roots). This will ensure less bugs and insects are present over time, and less fertilizer is needed.

3. <u>Reduce or replace lawn (if desired)</u> although this goes against the American culture of rich-green lawns. The need to take serious thought must be taken if water bill costs exceed the desired benefits of the lawn. The possible choice is a smaller section of lawn with multiple gardens laid out into a path, to stroll and enjoy.

4. <u>Plants of beauty and durability are</u> listed below by categories of Trees, shrubs, perennials, groundcover, grasses, ferns and vines. Each category is grouped by size and includes color, bloom time and fragrance and water habits, if applicable.

5. <u>Save your back low maintenance</u> is every gardener's chronic problem. The introduction of new gadgets on the market helps, but the back is very vulnerable. The solution is to create gardens which require lower maintenance and still have beauty. This allows the natural ecosystem of the plant community to adjust themselves by filling in by dying and new plants move in. The garden is self-sustaining within its community.

6. <u>Mulch</u> has many advantages to the Xeriscape. The moisture will be retained by the soil and not lost to transpiration to the air. In warmer climates mulch reduces water loss and in

colder climates it will protect the plants. The weeds will be kept down, so less weeding is needed. As time passes the mulch will decay into the soil and help build the soil. There are many types of mulch: shredded leaves, ground bark, stones and fabric (weed barrier). The acidity of some mulches must be checked for desired plants. Some mulches are higher in acidity than others, a word of advice according to Garden Gate: move the mulch away from the base of plants by a few inches in the summer.

7. <u>Thrifty irrigation and timing of watering</u>. Even with proper layout some watering is required. The rule is to water when less evaporation is lost from the plants. This is done by watering at sunrise or sunset. The general rule to tell if plants are in need of water is to plant indicator plants that wilt when water is needed. The best plant for this is ferns (see below). There are (4) water efficient systems on the market or available in your own home. The conventional oscillating sprinklers lose 50% of what is dispensed through evaporation. The adequate amount of water is one inch per week, as a rule of thumb.

   A.) Drip irrigation will distribute water to the plant roots is the most efficient way to water when rain is scarce. This can be done with modified plastic milk jugs. This is done by punching a hole in the bottom and sinking them into the soil next to the plant and filling as needed. The other method is using perforated plastic hoses with fittings and timers. The more refined the system the more efficient it works.

   B.) The old fashioned reservoirs "Cisterns" that our ancestors have used. This system captures rainwater runoff. This is well suited for the garden, but not suitable for drinking. The water is channeled from downspouts into drums, buckets or other holding tanks.

C.) The use of "Gray water" from household wastewater (bath showers, sinks and tubs) is a great source of nitrogen and phosphorus. These nutrients are lacking in sandy soils. The water must be used immediately and never stored. The only question in using this system is to check with your local town or city officials to determine if this is legal in your area. This water is not for vegetable gardens.

D.) The method used on golf courses and many municipal landscapers and a few gardeners is by adding absorbents. These polymer water absorbents have been on the market for approximately 15 years. The polymer works much like clay. The polymer particles become gelatinous when wet, and can hold 10 to 500 times their weight in water. The liquid polymers will biodegrade completely in five to ten years, according to the distributors. The use of this product will double the holding capacity of the soil and often double the root mass of the plants. This also reduces the transpiration in plants and will improve germination.

The cost savings of this method are worth the little patience and time spent to achieve a native, low-watering garden. The natural garden will also be enjoyed by birds and butterflies. The labor saved (and one's back) will be enjoyed for years to come. The satisfactions of watching the Xeriscape garden grow and decorate your yard.

DIANE M. GUIDEBECK

INDEX OF NATIVE SPECIES FOR XERISCAPING

* These are selections of non-native species which work in a Xeriscape Garden.

TREES

SHORT (less than 30')
- *Amelancier canadensis* (Downy Shadbush) - This grows in moist or dry conditions. Flowers in May and fruit are fleshy. Leaves densely white tomentose beneath at flowering time.
- *Amelanchier nantucketensis* (Nantucket Shadbush) - This grows in moist or dry conditions. Flowers in May and fruit are fleshy. Leaves shiny on top.
- *Acer pensylvanicum* (Striped Maple) – The bark is striped. This tree tolerates wind and salt spray and can be planted in full sun or partial shade.
- *Crategus punctata* (Dotted Hawthorn) – This thrives near the sea and in full sun. Thorns and dotted leaves.
- *Taxus canadensis* (Yew) – This tree requires some protection but will tolerate some exposure. Needs annual evergreen fertilizer application.

MODERATE (40' to 75')
- *Chamaecyparis thyoides* (White cedar) – Columnar with ascending branches, requires evergreen fertilizer application. Needs an open and protected area.
- *Ilex opaca* (American Holly) – Pyramidal shape with red fruit (June 14-26). This will tolerate salt spray but requires open and protected areas.

Pinus strobus (White Pine) – This requires well drained soil.

Quercus genus (Oak) – There are two varieties each with different bark styles. *Q. alba* (White Oak) with scaly bark appearance. *Q. rubra* (Red Oak) with ski track styled bark. *Q. veluntina* (Black Oak) with alligator bark pattern. *Q. coccinea* (Scarlet Oak) with finer bark pattern and lacy leaves.

Tillia americana (White Linden) – Pyramidal shape with dense growth. Requires rich soil. Flowers July 1 to August 1.

Thuja occidentalis (Arborvitae) – Columnar tree with ascending branches. This tree requires some protection but will tolerate some exposure. Needs annual evergreen fertilizer application.

Ulmus rubra (Slippery Elm) – Leaves are fragrant when dry.

TALL (greater than 75')

Fagus grandifolia (American Beech) – Bark gray, large leaves. Flowers May 7-30. Requires well prepared soil and large amounts of organic matter. This requires annual fertilizer.

Fraxinus americana (White Ash) – This tree tolerates poor soil, salt air and wind. Full sun.

Picea glauca (White Spruce) – This tree is a great wind breaker and is well situated in thin gravelly soil. Fruit in July.

PERENNIALS

I had a college professor that said weeds are nothing more than undesirable flowers.
Embrace all the beauty of any flower.

MODERATE (1' TO 2')

Achillea borealis (Yarrow) – Flowers white with clusters on erect fernlike foliage. Drought resistant. Full sun. Summer bloom.

Anemone cylindrica & *A. virginicana* (Anemone) – Pink, rose or white blossoms with yellow centers on medium green foliage. Needs moisture and moderate fertile soil. Partial shade or full sun. Blooms in the fall.

Aquilegia canadensis (Wild Columbine) – Variety of colors of delicate trumpet like flowers, fernlike foliage. Needs moisture and enriched soil. Partial shade or full sun. Early spring bloom.

Artemisia caudata (Dusty Miller or White Sage) – Silvery gray foliage. Plant in well drained sandy soil in full sun. Drought resistant. Blooms late summer.

Asclepias purpurascens (Purple Butterfly weed), *A. incartiata* (Flesh Butterfly weed) *A. tuberosa* (Orange Butterfly weed) – Umbels of flowers in midsummer on bright green foliage. Thrives in full sun and sandy soil. Drought resistant. All bloom during summer months.

Coreopsis rosea (Coreopsis) – Rose colored daisy like blooms on medium green foliage. Thrives in poor to ordinary soil. Full sun. Drought resistant. Flowers July 16 to September 19.

Eupatorium aromaticum (Hardy ageratum) – Fluffy pale purple blossoms on coarse hairy foliage. Thrives in well drained soil in full sun or partial shade. Needs moisture. Aromatic. Flowers August 8 to September 16.

Heuchera americana (Coralbells or Alumroot) – Red, pink or white bell-shaped flowers on spikes from medium-green or variegated foliage. Thrives in moderately fertile, rich sweet soils or dry soil. Full sun or partial shade. Rare.

Lilium philadephicum (Wood Lily) – Summer Bloom. Flowers limited and terminal with orange to reddish sepals. Stems leafy. Drought resistant

Lilium canadense (Canada Lily) – Yellow or orange flowers. Summer Bloom. Flowers limited and terminal with orange to reddish sepals. Stems leafy. Drought resistant

Limonium carolinianum (Sea Lavender) – Small lavender blossoms on spreading, silvery foliage. Thrives in well-drained soil or ordinary soil. Full sun. Drought resistant.

Monarda fistulosa (Wild Bergamot) – Lilac or pink 3" whorled petals on medium green foliage. Thrives in ordinary soil. Full sun or partial shade. Needs moisture.

Myosotis sylvatica (Forget – me – not) – Sky blue tiny flowers on medium green heart shaped foliage. Thrives in moderately fertile soil in partial or deep shade. Drought resistant.

This Photo by Unknown Author is licensed under CC BY-SA

Oenothera tetragona (Evening Primrose) – Various colors on medium foliage. Thrives in well drained sandy soil. Full sun. Drought resistant.

Polygonatum pubescens (Hairy/Small True Solomon) - the hairy Solomon's seal or downy Solomon's seal, is a species of flowering plant in the family Asparagaceae, native to the north-central and eastern US and eastern Canada. It is a forest gap specialist.

Rudbeckia serotina (Black Eyed Susan) – Yellow colored daisy like blossoms on medium foliage. Thrives in ordinary soil. Full sun. Drought resistant.

This Photo by Unknown Author is licensed under CC BY-NC

Rununcules genus (Crowfoot or Buttercup) – Variety of flower colors and sizes. Grows in a variety of soil conditions. Full sun or partial shade.

Smilacina andurat (False Solomon's Seal) – Wide leaves. Flowers are cream colored and fruit fleshy. Moist or dry woods. Spring blooms.

XERISCAPING & SUSTAINABILITY FOR NEW ENGLAND

Solidago canadensis (Goldenrod) – Golden plume like blossoms on medium green foliage. Thrives in well drained, ordinary soil. Full sun or partial shade. Summer bloom.

Veronica noveboracensis* (Speedwell) – Blue, lavender clusters of blossoms on lustrous foliage. Thrives in well drained, sandy soil. Full sun and some partial shade. Drought resistant. Repeated blooms if deadheaded. Flowers August 15 to September 13.

Verbena hastata (Blue Vervain) – Blue or pink spike like flowers on coarse foliage. Drought resistant. Works well with American Beach grass.

Viola andur (Bird's Foot Violet) – The leaves are deeply cut. Flowers are either white or purplish. Full sun to shade conditions. Drought resistant. Blooms in spring.

Viola fimbrelatula (Fringed Violet) – Flowers purple. Full sun to shade conditions. Drought resistant. Blooms in spring.

GROUNDCOVERS

SHORT (less than 6")

Achillea tomentosa* (Wooly Yarrow) – Yellow dense structured flowers on fernlike foliage. Thrives in enriched sandy soil. Full sun. Drought resistant. Repeated blooms if deadheaded.

Cornus canadensis (Bunchberry) – Yellow blossoms with white bracts. Fruit is red. Spring blooming. Requires moisture and organic soil. Partial shade.

Gaultheria procumbens (Wintergreen) - Creeping evergreen and scarlet fruits. Very small white flowers in spring. Shiny dark green leaves. Thrives in partial shade and moist sandy soil. Aromatic leaves. Edible fruit.

This Photo by Unknown Author is licensed under CC BY

Hypericum canadense (Saint- Johnswort) – Large, bright yellow blossoms. Thrives in full sun and in sandy soil. Late summer bloom. Drought resistant.

Phlox andurat* (Moss pink) – Small pine clustered blooms, semi-green foliage. Thrives in ordinary soil. Full sun or partial shade. Drought resistant. Mid-spring blooms.

Vinca minor* (Creeping Myrtle) – Small medium blue flowers on glossy foliage. Creeping growth. Thrives in ordinary soil. Full sun, partial shade and deep shade. Drought resistant.

This Photo by Unknown Author is licensed under CC BY-SA

MODERATE (6" to 1')

Cerastium tomentosum* (Snow in summer) – White blossoms on woolly gray foliage. Thrives in poor soil and pure sand. Full sun. Blooms in June.

Iberis sempervirens* (Candytuft) – Clustered white blossoms on needlelike, evergreen foliage. Thrives in ordinary soil. Full sun. Drought resistant.

Opuntia humifusa (Prickly pear) – One large yellow flowers on thorny cactus foliage. Thrives in sandy soil. Full sun. Drought resistant.

Phlox andurat (Spotted Wild Sweet William Phlox) – Purple flowers on matted foliage. Full sun. Drought resistant. Blooms in spring.

TALL (greater than 1')

Arabis canadensis (Rock cress) – White clustered flowers on silver-green foliage. Thrives in ordinary, gritty, well drained soil. Full sun. Drought resistant. Summer blooms.

Arctostaphylos Uva-ursi (Bearberry) – Evergreen foliage turning bronze in fall with red berries. Thrives in poor, sandy soil. Full sun. Drought resistant.

Arenaria lateriflora (Grove Sandwort) – White star like blossoms on moss like foliage. Thrives in ordinary soil. Full sun or partial shade. Drought resistant.

Artemisia stellerana* (Beach wormwood) – Silvery plant with yellow clustered flowers. Thrives in poor sandy soil. Full sun Drought resistant (hates water). *A. canadensis* is rare so this is a good substitute.

Erica carnea * (Spring Heath) – Spiked white flowers on evergreen foliage. Thrives in poor soil. Full sun or partial shade. Blooms in spring.

Euonymus andura (Winter Creeper) – Deep green evergreen foliage. Fruiting in summer and fall with pale red fruit. Thrives in poor soil. Full sun or partial shade. Drought resistant.

Lamium maculatum* (Dead Nettle) – Clustered white blossoms on silvery-white, variegated foliage. Thrives in ordinary soil. Light shade. Drought resistant.

Polemonium caeruleum * (Jacob's ladder) – Small, cup shaped blue flowers on mounded foliage. Thrives in average soil. Full sun or shade. Drought resistant.

Sedum hispanicum (Stonecrop) – Variety of flower colors on a variety of foliage colors. Flowers turn vibrant colors in the fall. Full sun. Drought resistant.

Sempervivum* (Hens and chicks) – Foliage of various colors and strange flowers in early summer. Thrives in ordinary soil. Full sun. Drought resistant.

FERNS

Adiantum pedatum (Maidenhair) – Soft, lacy green foliage. Requires moist well drained foliage. Light to deep shade. 18 – 24"

Athyrium filix-femina (Lady fern) – Yellow-green foliage and deeply cut. Requires ordinary moist soil. Partial shade. 24 – 48"

Matteuccia struthipteris* (Ostrich fern) -Yellow-green feathery fronds. Requires rich soil with organic matter. Partial shade. 3 – 6'

Osmunda cinnamomea (Cinnamon fern) – Waxy, textured and deep green fronds on cinnamon-colored stalks. Requires rich soil with organic matter. Light to deep shade. 3 4 '

Osmunda regalis (Royal fern) – Deep Forest green foliage. Requires slightly acidic soil and moisture. Deep to light shade. 4 – 6'

XERISCAPING & SUSTAINABILITY FOR NEW ENGLAND

GRASSES

- *Ammophila breviligulata* (American Beach grass) – Narrow whiplike leaves. Requires sandy soil or dunes. Full sun. Drought resistant. 12"
- *Festuca rubra* (Red Fescue) – Mass growing in tufts. Thrives in ordinary soil. Requires water only during severe drought conditions. 8"
- *Holcus lanatus** (Variegated Velvet grass) – Green and white leaves. Mass growing. Tolerates sandy soil. Drought resistant. 8"
- *Panicum virgatum* (Switchgrass) – Delicately cut foliage with cloudlike blooms. Thrives in ordinary soil. Full sun. Blooms from midsummer to fall. Requires some watering. 4–7'.
- *Pennisetum alopecuroides* (Fountain grass) – Finely arching foliage with rose-tan foxtail shaped blooms. Thrives in sandy soil. Full sun. Requires some watering. 3 – 4'

This Photo by Unknown Author is licensed under CC BY-SA

VINES (Most are invasive, please check with your local extension service to determine invasiveness.)

Celastrus scandens (American Bittersweet) – Berries of orange and red appear in the fall. Thrives in ordinary soil. Full sun or partial shade. Drought resistant.

Clematis virginiana, C. dioscoreifolia C. verticillaris, C. robusta (Clematis) – Variety of large flowers colors with saucerlike blossoms. Foliage varies and can be glossy. Thrives in moderate fertile soil and slightly alkaline soil. Full sun or partial shade. Requires moisture during summer drought. Fragrant 3 – 30'

Ipomoea andurate (Morning glory) – Annual. Various colors of blooms with large heart shaped foliage. Thrives in ordinary soil. Full sun. Requires moisture. Summer bloom.

Lonicera sempervivens (Trumpet Honeysuckle) – Evergreen. Delicate, fragrant spiderlike flowers of various colors on compact vines of medium foliage. Thrive in ordinary soil. Full sun. Drought resistant. Summer bloom.

This Photo by Unknown Author is licensed under CC BY-SA

Lonicera canadensis (American Flyhigh Honeysuckle) – Evergreen. Delicate, fragrant spiderlike flowers of various colors on compact vines of medium foliage. Thrive in ordinary soil. Full sun. Drought resistant. Spring bloom.

Smilax glauca (Sawbrier) – Semi evergreen foliage with leaves bearing blue-black berries in the fall. Thrives in ordinary soil. Light conditions. Drought resistant. Early summer bloom.

Smilax hervacea (Jacob's Ladder) – Semi evergreen foliage with leaves bearing blue-black berries in the fall. Thrives in ordinary soil. Light conditions. Drought resistant. Early summer bloom. This is not the same as *Polemonium caeruleum*.

This Photo by Unknown Author is licensed under CC BY

SHRUBS

Baccharis halimifolia (Sea myrtle) – Deciduous. White thistlelike blossoms on coarse yellow-green foliage. Highly tolerant of salt spray and sandy soil. Drought resistant. 4 – 10'

Clethra alnifolia (Sweet Pepperbush) – Deciduous. Spiked blooms of white with black seeds on medium-green foliage. Thrives in wet or sandy soil and tolerates salt spray. Full sun or partial shade. Fragrant. Late summer bloom.

Cornus stolonifera (Red osier Dogwood) – Deciduous. Small white blossoms in late spring and white berries in summer. Red bark. 7'

Gaylussacia baccata (Black Huckleberry) – Deciduous. Red like flowers succeeded by dark blue berries. Small green leaves which turn red in the fall. Thrives in wet or dry sandy soil. Drought resistant.

Juniperus horizontalis (Horizontal Juniper) – Coniferous, creeping and low spreading. Variety of shapes and color. Very tolerant of sandy soil and conditions.

Prunus maritima (Beach plum) – Deciduous, dense and compact foliage with white flowers in the spring. In the fall small blue to red plums. Leaves turn red in the fall. Thrives in sandy soil, shade, wind and salt spray. Drought resistant.

This Photo by Unknown Author is licensed under CC BY-NC-ND

Spiraea alba (Bridal wreath or Meadow Sweet) – Deciduous. Arching branches covered completely covered blossoms of various colors in the late spring. Full sun. Requires watering.

Vaccunium corymbosum (Highbush blueberry) – Deciduous White flowers followed by blueberries in the early summer. Foliage turns red in the fall. Drought resistant and adapted to wetland conditions.

DIANE M. GUIDEBECK

APPENDEX

Average Annual Extreme
Minimum Temperature
1976-2005

Temp (F)	Zone	Temp (C)
-60 to -55	1a	-51.1 to -48.3
-55 to -50	1b	-48.3 to -45.6
-50 to -45	2a	-45.6 to -42.8
-45 to -40	2b	-42.8 to -40
-40 to -35	3a	-40 to -37.2
-35 to -30	3b	-37.2 to -34.4
-30 to -25	4a	-34.4 to -31.7
-25 to -20	4b	-31.7 to -28.9
-20 to -15	5a	-28.9 to -26.1
-15 to -10	5b	-26.1 to -23.3
-10 to -5	6a	-23.3 to -20.6
-5 to 0	6b	-20.6 to -17.8
0 to 5	7a	-17.8 to -15
5 to 10	7b	-15 to -12.2
10 to 15	8a	-12.2 to -9.4
15 to 20	8b	-9.4 to -6.7
20 to 25	9a	-6.7 to -3.9
25 to 30	9b	-3.9 to -1.1
30 to 35	10a	-1.1 to 1.7
35 to 40	10b	1.7 to 4.4
40 to 45	11a	4.4 to 7.2
45 to 50	11b	7.2 to 10
50 to 55	12a	10 to 12.8
55 to 60	12b	12.8 to 15.6
60 to 65	13a	15.6 to 18.3
65 to 70	13b	18.3 to 21.1

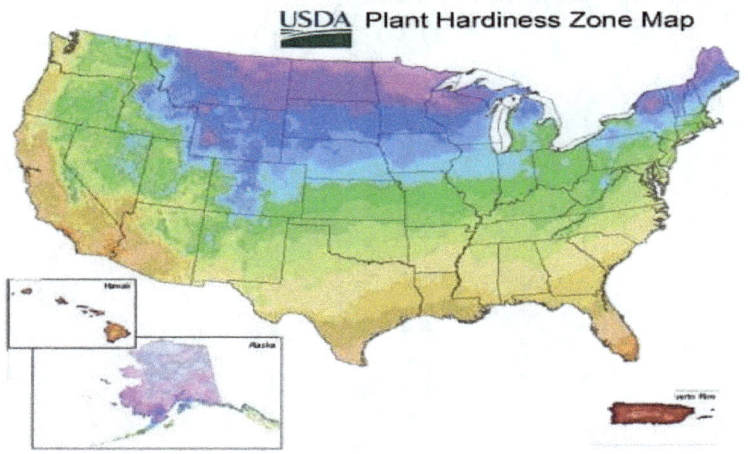

USDA Plant Hardiness Zone Map

This Photo by Unknown Author is licensed under CC BY-NC

XERISCAPING & SUSTAINABILITY FOR NEW ENGLAND

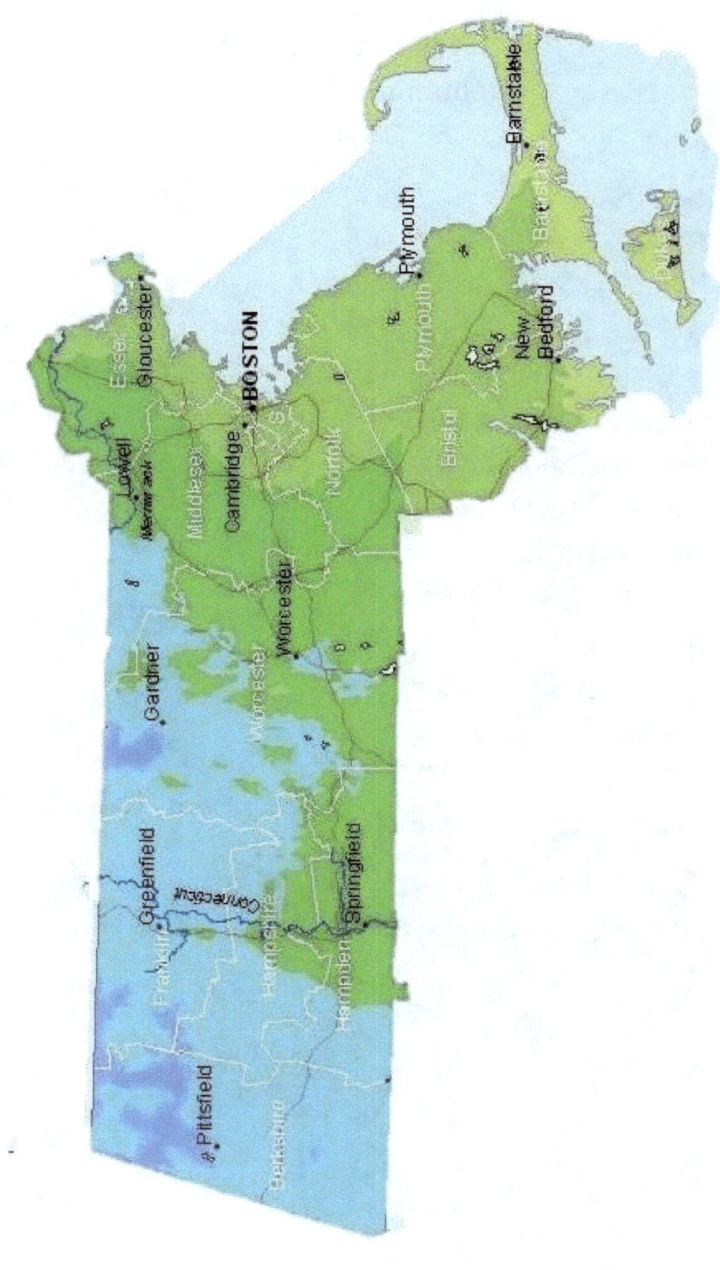

DIANE M. GUIDEBECK

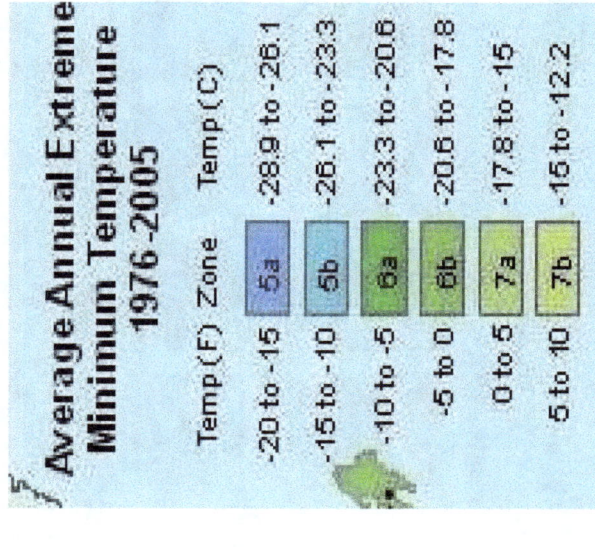

This Photo by Unknown Author is licensed under CC BY

XERISCAPING & SUSTAINABILITY FOR NEW ENGLAND

There are many online tools available.
Embrace them.

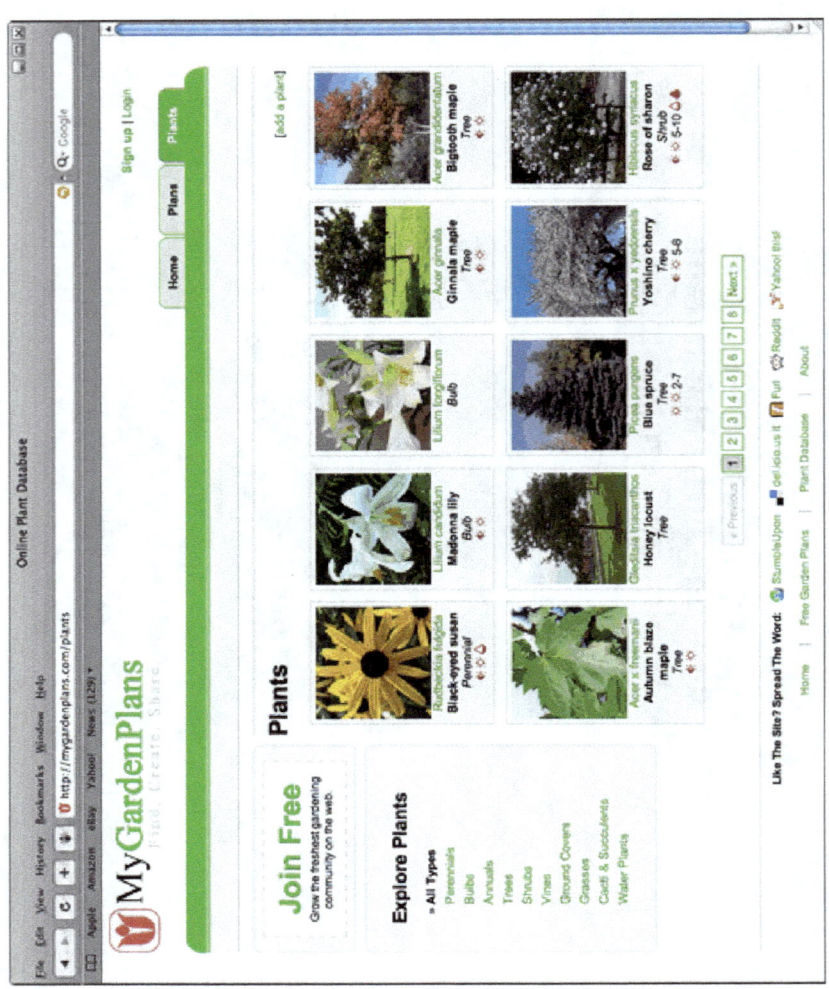

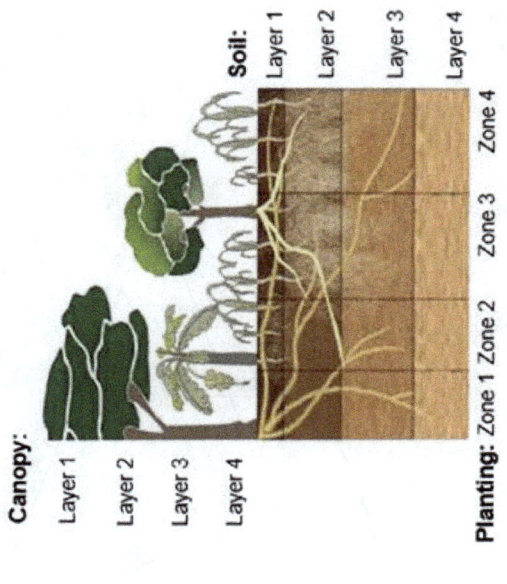

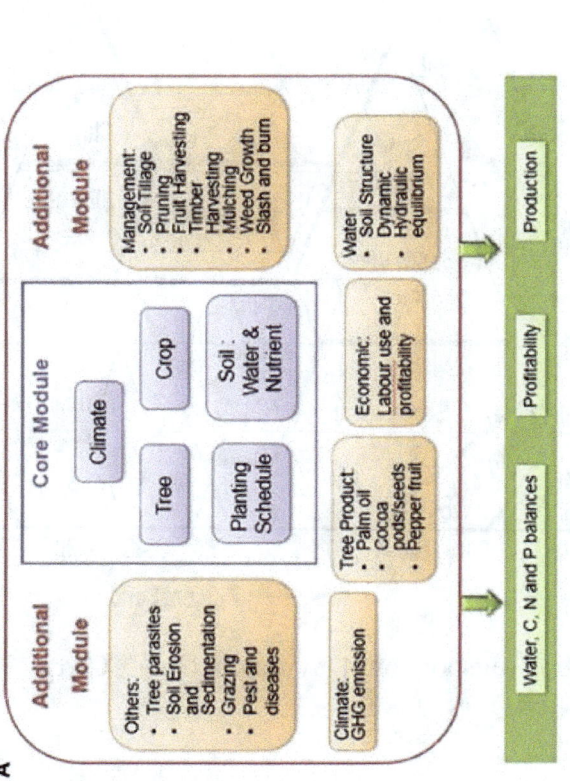

This Photo by Unknown Author is licensed under CC BY

Soil Triangle

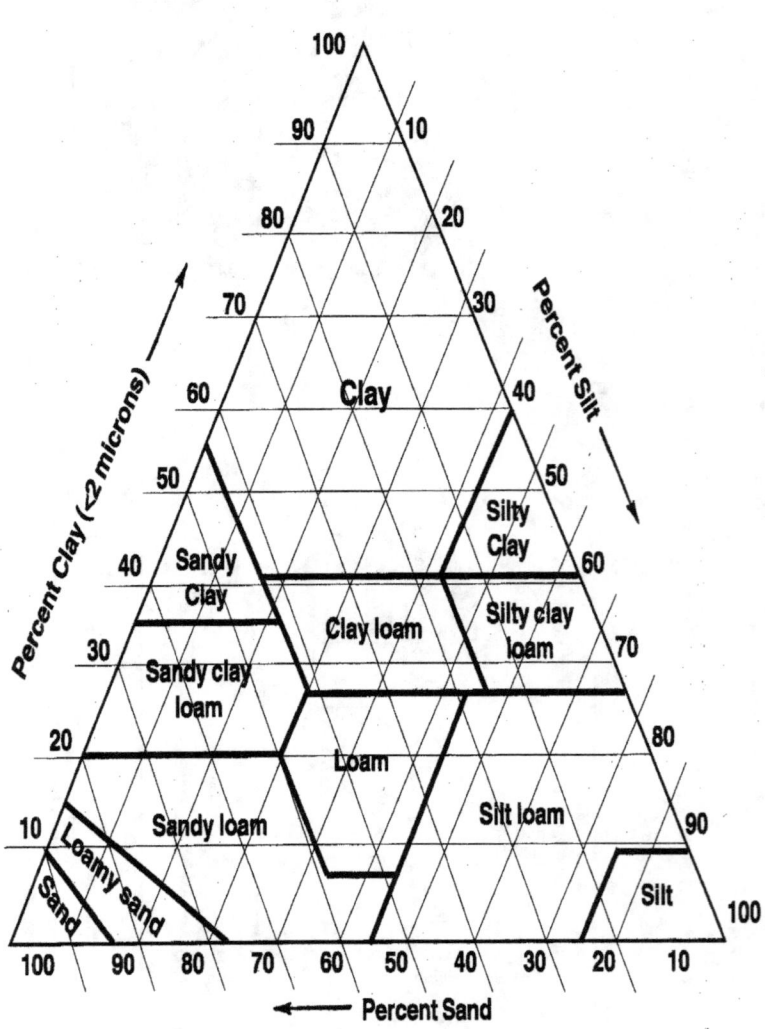

http://4.bp.blogspot.com/DhvuwoPwUnQ/TCKqfC3bPII/AAA
AAAAAARQ/vS19b80N7…...

DIANE M. GUIDEBECK

Layering plants allows for a variety of colors
and gives the garden a natural look.

This Photo by Unknown Author is licensed under CC BY-NC

XERISCAPING & SUSTAINABILITY FOR NEW ENGLAND

Consider the seasons of New England
and embrace the bold colors of autumn.

This Photo by Unknown Author is licensed under CC BY-NC-ND

DIANE M. GUIDEBECK

Wooded areas can also have
depth and dimension.

This Photo by Unknown Author is licensed under CC BY-NC-ND

XERISCAPING & SUSTAINABILITY FOR NEW ENGLAND

Hydrangeas come in many varieties.

Ph in the soil impacts the color.

Speak to your local garden center about different options.

When planning, be attentive to the height and width of a mature plant.

This Photo by Unknown Author is licensed under CC BY-SA-NC

Ph Chart

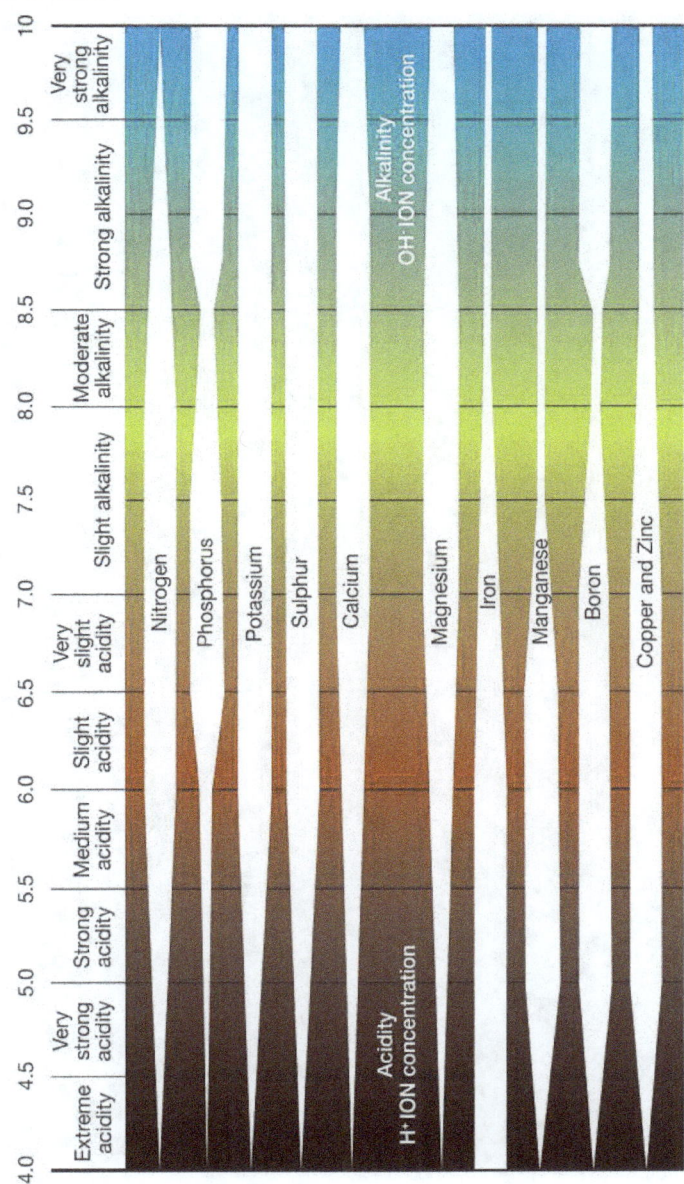

Samples from my personal portfolio

DIANE M. GUIDEBECK

XERISCAPING & SUSTAINABILITY FOR NEW ENGLAND

DIANE M. GUIDEBECK

XERISCAPING & SUSTAINABILITY FOR NEW ENGLAND

DIANE M. GUIDEBECK

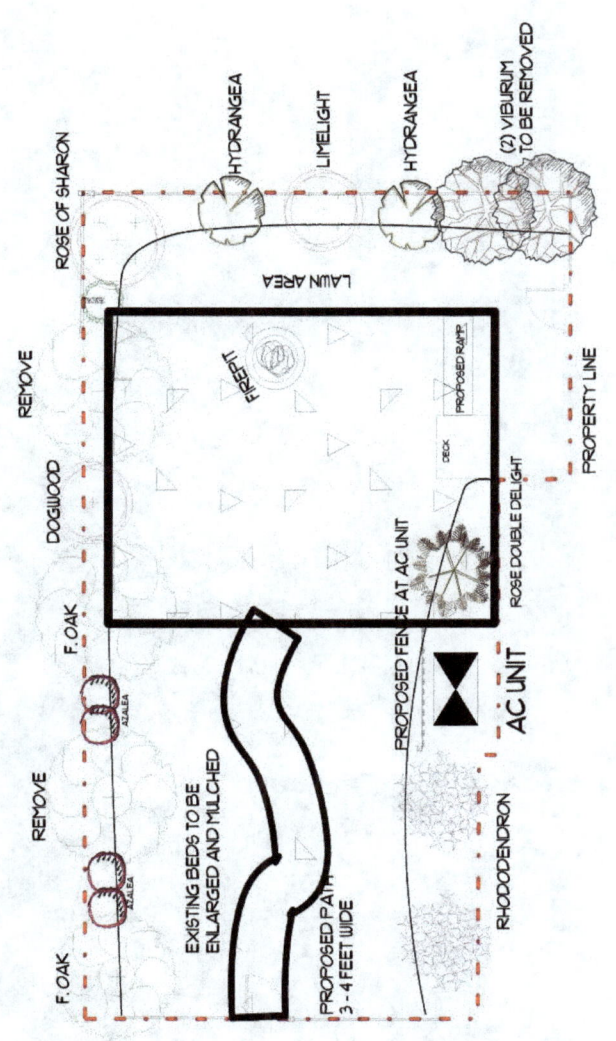

XERISCAPING & SUSTAINABILITY FOR NEW ENGLAND

DIANE M. GUIDEBECK

XERISCAPING & SUSTAINABILITY FOR NEW ENGLAND

www.ingramcontent.com/pod-product-compliance
Lightning Source LLC
LaVergne TN
LVHW050557090426
835512LV00008B/1215